# Knowledge
# MASTERS

# OUTER SPACE

Written by
**Harry Ford and Kay Barnham**

Harry Ford is a lecturer at the Caird Planetarium, the Old Royal Observatory, National Maritime Museum, where he regularly answers children's questions. Formerly curator of the Mills Observatory, Dundee, Scotland, he and his wife Lynne built the Planetarium at the Central Museum, Southend. In 1985, he was awarded the Lorimer Gold Medal of the Astronomical Society of Edinburgh, Scotland.

Published by
Alligator Books Limited
Gadd House, Arcadia Avenue
London N3 2JU

Printed in China

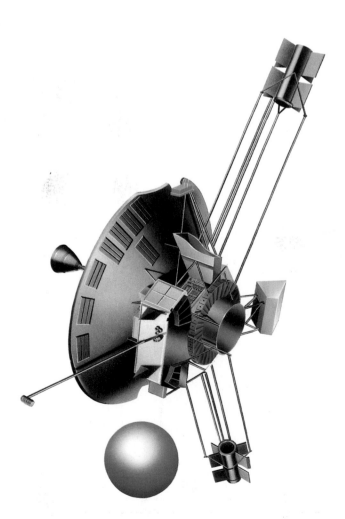

# Contents

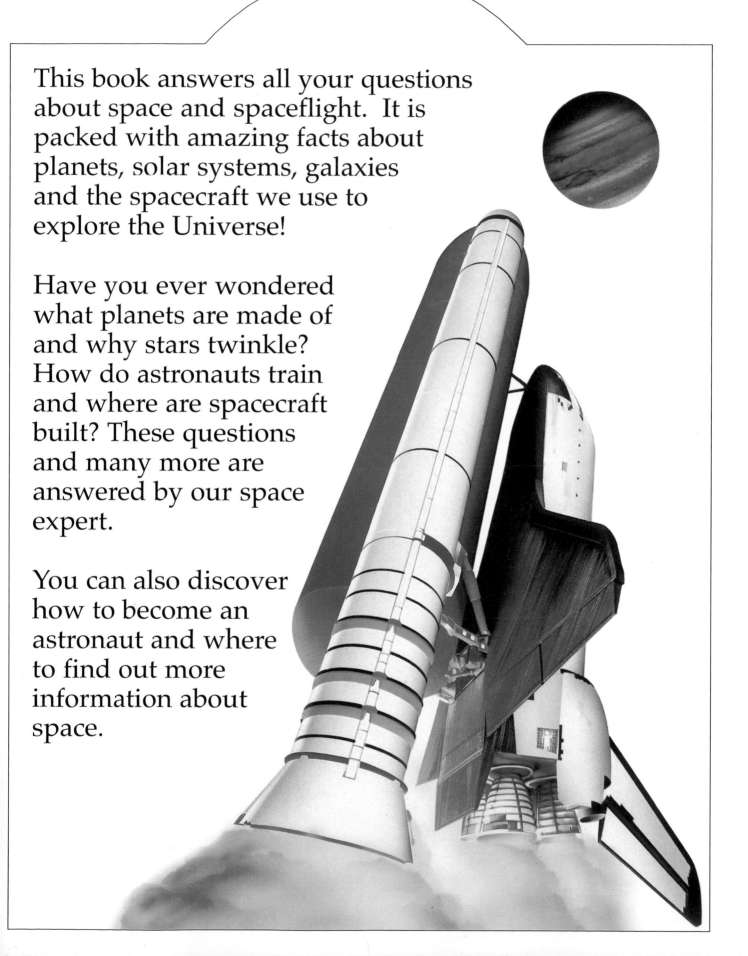

This book answers all your questions about space and spaceflight. It is packed with amazing facts about planets, solar systems, galaxies and the spacecraft we use to explore the Universe!

Have you ever wondered what planets are made of and why stars twinkle? How do astronauts train and where are spacecraft built? These questions and many more are answered by our space expert.

You can also discover how to become an astronaut and where to find out more information about space.

**4**

Scientists think that the Universe may contain huge amounts of invisible material called dark matter.

# What is space?

S pace is the name we give to the region beyond our planet, Earth, which may stretch on forever. Space is made of nothing at all, but it has lots of things in it, such as planets and stars. Space and its contents are called the Universe.

**Q How was the Universe made?**

**A** Many scientists believe that the Universe is the result of an explosion called the Big Bang, which occurred about 14 billion years ago.

**Q What was the Big Bang?**

**A** The Big Bang was an explosion of all the matter in the Universe, which was squashed into a tiny area at more than 10 billion°C. The matter exploded so quickly that, within a hundredth of a second, the Universe was as big as the Sun! It carried on growing.

**Q Is there anything left of the Big Bang?**

**A** Scientists have found that the average temperature of the Universe is 3°C above absolute zero, which is the coldest temperature possible. This heat could come from the Big Bang continuing to slow down.

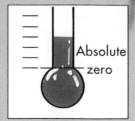

Absolute zero

**Q Is the Universe still getting bigger?**

**A** Yes. Scientists have discovered that matter and groups of stars are still moving further away from each other. However, they are now moving much more slowly than just after the Big Bang.

In 1929, Edwin Hubble discovered that the Universe was getting bigger. This led to the Big Bang theory.

Stars would explode if gravity were not holding their material together.

**Q How do we measure large distances in space?**

**A** Other stars and planets are so far away that if we measured the distance in kilometres, the number would be enormous. Instead, scientists measure these huge distances in light years. Light travels at 300 km per second, so a light year is the distance light travels in one year - 9,460,000,000,000 km!

**Q What is the Universe made of?**

**A** Everything in the Universe is made of atoms. When the Universe had cooled down after the Big Bang, tiny particles called protons, electrons and neutrons formed. These particles joined together in different ways to make up different sorts of atoms. For example, a helium atom is made up of two electrons, two protons and two neutrons.

**Q How were stars and planets formed?**

**A** Atoms have gravity, which means that they pull things towards them. After the Big Bang, gravity made atoms clump together to form stars and planets. Stars are made of hydrogen and helium atoms. Solid planets are made of carbon and iron atoms.

**Q How big is the Universe?**

**A** Scientists do not know how big the Universe is. So far, their instruments have been able to see as far as 10,000 million light years into space, where there is a long line of galaxies. (A galaxy is a group of stars.) Scientists do not yet know what is beyond!

Scientists who study stars and planets are called astronomers.

# What is a galaxy?

**A** galaxy is a group of millions of stars. A spiral galaxy looks like a huge, spinning Catherine wheel. Most of the stars are in the centre, with trailing spiral arms of stars around the outside.

**Q** What is the Milky Way?

**A** The Milky Way is the name of our galaxy. It is a spiral galaxy and our Solar System is in one of its spiral arms. The centre of the Milky Way can sometimes be spotted at night. It looks like a misty streak across the sky.

**Q** How many galaxies are there in Universe?

**A** There may be 100 billion galaxies!

**Q** Which is the biggest galaxy?

**A** The Andromeda Galaxy is the biggest galaxy of those near the Milky Way. On a clear night, all you can see of this galaxy is a small fuzzy blob, but it has twice as many stars as the Milky Way - perhaps as many as 200 billion! There may be galaxies even bigger than Andromeda.

**Q** When were galaxies discovered?

**A** The first astronomers called misty patches in the sky nebulae, which means mist. It was not until early this century that it was found that many of these mysterious nebulae were actually distant galaxies.

The Milky Way measures about 946,000,000,000,000,000 km, or 100,000 light years across.

The ancient Greeks gave the Milky Way its name because they thought it was made of drops of milk from the breasts of the goddess Hera.

**Q** What is at the centre of the Milky Way?

**A** Scientists have discovered that there is a huge amount of hot gas at the centre of our galaxy. Some experts think that this may be caused by a enormous, swirling black hole which is slowly sucking in dust, gas and even light. You can find out more about black holes on page 21.

There are millions of spiral galaxies in the Universe. These galaxies contain many young stars.

**Q** Are galaxies evenly spread throughout space?

**A** There are enormous distances between galaxies, but scientists think that they are grouped in clusters. There may be thousands of galaxies in each cluster. Clusters of galaxies may, in turn, be grouped in superclusters.

**Q** Are all galaxies shaped like the Milky Way?

**A** No. Galaxies can also be shaped like barred spirals and ellipses. Other galaxies have no definite shape.

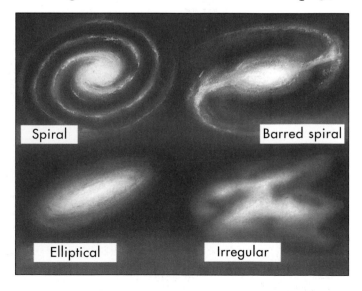

Spiral

Barred spiral

Elliptical

Irregular

# What is a solar system?

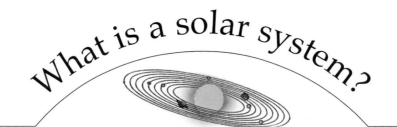

**A** solar system is a group of planets and moons which travel round, or orbit, a star. Every star is actually a sun, which may have its own solar system.

**Q** What are the planets in our Solar System called?

**A** The nine planets which orbit our Sun are called Mercury, Venus, Earth, Mars, Jupiter, Saturn, Uranus, Neptune and Pluto.

**Q** How old is the Solar System?

**A** Our Solar System was formed about 4.6 billion years ago, nearly 10 billion years after the Universe began. New stars and solar systems are still being formed!

**Q** How long does it take each planet to orbit the Sun?

**A** It takes Earth a year to travel once around the Sun. Planets nearer the Sun take less time and planets further away take longer. The table below shows how long it takes each planet to orbit the Sun.

**Q** Can we see any planets from Earth without a telescope?

**A** The five planets nearest to Earth can be seen with the naked eye. These are Mercury, Venus, Mars, Jupiter and Saturn. They were first sighted in prehistoric times.

Saturn

Uranus

Neptune

Pluto

| Mercury | 87.97 days |
| --- | --- |
| Venus | 224.70 days |
| Earth | 365.26 days |
| Mars | 686.98 days |
| Jupiter | 11.86 years |
| Saturn | 29.50 years |
| Uranus | 84.01 years |
| Neptune | 164.79 years |
| Pluto | 248.54 years |

Ganymede is the biggest moon in our Solar System. It measures 5,260 km across and orbits Jupiter.

The planets in our Solar System are named after the Roman gods. Mars was the god of war.

**Q** **What is the difference between a planet and a moon?**

**A** Planets orbit suns, while moons orbit planets.

**Q** **Are there any other planets in our Solar System beyond Pluto?**

**A** So far, six tiny planets have been found. The first two have been named Smiley and Karla. Scientists once hoped that a large planet would be discovered, but now it seems unlikely.

**Q** **Do other planets have moons?**

**A** Yes. Most planets have moons. Saturn has 19 moons, Jupiter and Uranus have 16 each, Neptune has 6, Mars has 2 and Pluto has only 1 moon.

Here you can see the Sun and planets in our Solar System (not to scale).

Mars

Earth

Venus

Mercury

Jupiter

Sun

# What is the Sun?

Before clocks were invented, people used sundials to tell what time of day it was.

**T**he Sun is a star. It is a great, glowing ball of hydrogen and helium gas. Without the Sun's light and heat, nothing could survive on Earth.

**Q** How hot is the Sun?

**A** The Sun is very hot indeed! Its surface is 6,000°C, and the temperature at the centre measures 14 million°C!

Sunspots are cooler areas on the sun's surface. Some are bigger than Earth.

**Q** Is Earth bigger than the Sun?

**A** No. Although, the Sun looks quite small to us, it is actually one million times bigger than our planet, Earth.

● Earth ◄─── The Sun is 149,600,000 km from Earth. ───► Sun

**Q** How do the Sun's rays affect Earth?

**A** Without the Sun's rays, life on Earth would die. Plants need the Sun's light to change carbon dioxide and water into the food they need. In turn, humans and animals rely on plants for their food supply.

This is a close-up view of the Sun.

A white dwarf star is a star that has used up its hydrogen fuel.

White dwarf

You must NEVER use a telescope or binoculars to look directly at the Sun - its light could blind you.

**Q** **Will the Sun last for ever?**

**A** It will last for many millions of years! In about 5 billion years' time, the Sun will have burnt up all of its hydrogen fuel. It will become a hundred times as bright as it is now, and swell up to swallow the nearest planets, including Earth. After another 100 million years, the Sun will shrink to become a white dwarf star.

Solar flares are huge clouds of glowing gases which loop above the Sun's surface.

**Q** **Is the Sun moving?**

**A** Yes. All the planets in our Solar System orbit the Sun and, in turn, our Solar System orbits the centre of our galaxy, the Milky Way. It takes about 225 million years, or one cosmic year, for the Sun and nine planets to travel around the Milky Way once.

The Sun in the Milky Way (not to scale)

**Q** **Can the Sun's rays be harmful?**

**A** We receive the Sun's light and heat, but most of the dangerous rays, such as ultra violet rays, are stopped by the layers of gas in Earth's atmosphere. However, the ozone layer is getting thinner. Scientists believe that it is being damaged by chemicals from Earth.

---------- The ozone layer

**Q** **Can spacecraft get close to the Sun?**

**A** The Sun is so hot that spacecraft cannot fly very near it. In 1976 *Helios 2* travelled to within 45,000,000 km of the Sun. This is closer than the Sun's nearest planet, Mercury.

Helios 2

Venus is always surrounded by clouds of sulphuric acid.

## What are planets made of?

Venus

**L**ike Earth, most of the smaller planets in our Solar System have a solid surface made of rock. However, Jupiter, Saturn, Uranus and Neptune, the four biggest planets, are made of gases!

**Q** Could we breathe on any other planet in our Solar System?

**A** No. One of Saturn's moons, Titan, may have an atmosphere made of nitrogen gas (which makes up four-fifths of Earth's atmosphere). However, to stay alive, human beings also need oxygen.

**Q** Is there life on other planets?

**A** All of the planets in the Solar System have been explored with telescopes and space probes. So far, nothing living has been found. The other planets in our system all seem to be too hot, too cold, or made entirely of gases.

**Q** Are there mountains, valleys and volcanoes on other planets?

**A** Yes. Most solid planets have geographical features like Earth. Scientists have found deserts, polar areas, mountains and valleys on Mars. Volcanoes have been found on Venus, Mars and Io (one of Jupiter's moons). The biggest volcano, Mount Olympus is on Mars. It is 25 km high!

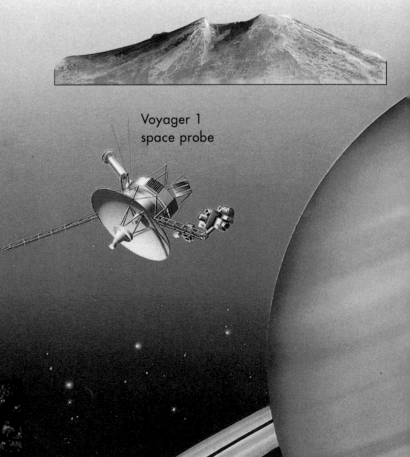

Voyager 1
space probe

Telescope

Space observatory

The Great Red Spot on Jupiter's surface is a furious storm.

Saturn's rings can be spotted even with a small telescope.

**Q** **Why is Mars red?**

**A** Mars is red because it is rusty! The surface of the planet is covered in iron oxide, or rust, which forms when iron mixes with small amounts of oxygen and water.

**Q** **Why does Saturn have stripes?**

**A** Saturn's atmosphere is made of different gases. Some of these gases do not mix and when Saturn spins, high winds blow the gases around the planet into stripes. Each stripe is a different kind of gas.

**Q** **What shape are planets?**

**A** A planet may look round, but it is actually shaped like a spheroid. This means that it looks like a squashed ball. Saturn and Jupiter spin very quickly, so they are the most squashed looking.

Saturn's rings

Saturn

**Q** **What are Saturn's rings made of?**

**A** They are made of millions of dust and ice particles. There are so many of them that the rings look solid. The rings shine because the ice particles in them reflect light.

## Could people live on the Moon?

An astronaut last walked on the Moon in 1973.

**T**here is no atmosphere on the Moon, so you would not be able to breathe. It is possible to set up scientific bases there, but anyone walking around on the Moon would need a space suit.

**Q** Why is the Moon covered in craters?

**A** Most of the Moon's craters were caused about three billion years ago by meteorites. These lumps of rock and iron hurtled through Space and crashed into the Moon at high speed.

**Q** What are the dark areas on the Moon?

**A** When people first looked through telescopes at the Moon, they thought that the dark areas were seas. They gave them names, such as the Sea of Tranquility. It was later discovered that these seas were really areas of dry, dark lava from volcanic eruptions.

**Q** Why isn't Earth covered with craters ?

**A** Earth was once covered with craters, but most have been worn away by rain, wind and movement of the Earth's crust There is no weather on the Moon, so its craters have not been worn away.

The Moon is bigger than the planet Pluto.

Pluto

Moon

The Moon is about 384,400 km from Earth. It would take you more than 9 years to walk there!

**Q** | **What is an eclipse of the Sun?**

**A** | This is when the Moon is directly between Earth and the Sun. For a few moments, the Sun's light is blocked and the Moon casts a shadow onto Earth, turning day into night!

An eclipse of the Sun

**Q** | **What happens when there is an eclipse of the Moon?**

**A** | This is when Earth is directly between the Moon and the Sun. We can only see the Moon because it reflects the Sun's light. If Earth travels between the Sun and the Moon, it stops the Sun's light reaching the Moon, so the Moon seems to disappear.

**Q** | **Why does the Moon seem to change shape?**

**A** | The Sun's light only falls on one side of the Moon. It takes 27.3 days, or one lunar month, for the Moon to orbit Earth. As the Moon orbits Earth, we see different amounts of the sunlit side of the Moon. When we can see all of the sunlit side, there is a full moon.

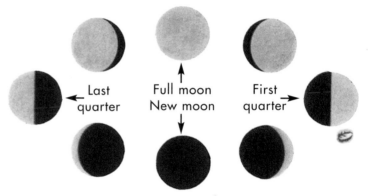

← Last quarter

Full moon
New moon

First quarter →

**Q** | **Does the Moon affect Earth?**

**A** | Yes. The Moon has its own gravity, which pulls Earth's seas towards it, making them bulge. As the Earth spins, the bulge moves around its surface. When the Moon is overhead, the sea reaches its highest level. When the Moon is over the coast, there is a high tide.

The Sun's gravity also has a small effect on Earth's seas. When the Sun and Moon both pull at once, there is a very high tide. This is called a spring tide.

The word comet means 'hairy star'.

# What is an asteroid belt?

**T**here are thousands of pieces of rock, called asteroids, in orbit around the Sun. Most of these asteroids are grouped together between Mars and Jupiter. These large groups of rocks are known as asteroid belts.

**Q** What are comets made of?

**A** Comets are huge balls of shining, frozen rock, gas and dust. The comet has a tail made of gas and dust which blows out from it in the solar wind sent out by the Sun. There may be as many as 100 billion comets orbiting the Sun.

**Q** How big are comets?

**A** The Giotto space probe showed that the head of Halley's Comet was as large as a mountain. A comet's tail can be over 100 million km long!

**Q** How did Halley's Comet get its name?

**A** In the 1600s, the brilliant scientist Edmond Halley realised that one particular comet orbited the Sun every 76 years. He correctly predicted that its next appearance would be in 1758. It will next be seen in 2062.

When lots of dust hits Earth's atmosphere, it burns up, and looks like lots of shooting stars. This is called a meteor shower.

A meteorite is a meteor that has fallen to Earth.

**Q** **Did an asteroid kill the last of the dinosaurs?**

**A** Perhaps. An asteroid which might have been as large as 10 km across fell near Yucatan, in Mexico, about 65 million years ago. The Chicxlub crater made by this asteroid is 180 km across. The force of the blast caused tidal waves and earthquakes and threw huge clouds of dust into the sky. Scientists think that all land animals that weighed over 30 kg died, including the last of the dinosaurs.

**Q** **What are shooting stars?**

**A** Shooting stars are not stars at all! They are actually tiny pieces of dust, called meteors. When a comet flies past, dust from its burning tail falls towards Earth. When these particles of dust hit Earth's atmosphere at very high speed, they burn up. On Earth, this looks as if a star is falling from the sky.

**Q** **Which is the biggest asteroid in our Solar System?**

**A** Asteroids are bigger than meteors and are like small planets. The largest asteroid in our Solar System is Ceres, which is over 1,000 km wide.

The force of the meteorite explosion in Siberia created such strong winds, that a farmer 200 km away was almost blown over.

**Q** **When was the last time a large meteor hit Earth?**

**A** The last time this happened was in 1908 in a remote area of Siberia, Russia. Great areas of trees were knocked down by the blast.

## Why do stars twinkle?

The nearest star to our Sun is Proxima Centauri, which is 4.3 light years or 40,678 billion km away.

**S**tars twinkle because the light they send towards Earth is bent by air currents moving about in our atmosphere. If you were to travel above Earth's atmosphere, the stars would not twinkle at all!

**Q** Why do stars shine?

**A** Stars shine because they are hot, just like our Sun. Inside a star, hydrogen gas turns into helium gas, which gives out energy in the form of light, heat and other invisible rays.

**Q** Can we tell the time by the stars?

**A** Yes. Earth spins around once every 24 hours. During the night, stars appears to move across the sky. It is possible to tell the time when their changing positions are measured. Before clocks, stars were an important way of telling the time at night.

**Q** Where is the best place to see stars?

**A** Bright stars can be seen easily from anywhere on clear nights, but the best place to see the dimmer stars is in the countryside. In towns, artificial light from street lighting fills the sky, making it difficult to see the dimmer stars.

The Sun is so far away that its light takes 8 minutes to reach us on Earth.

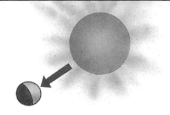

A star is formed in our galaxy every 18 days. That means there are 20 new stars each year!

**Q** What is the best time of night to see stars?

**A** The best time to see stars is when the sky is at its darkest. This is at midnight, when the Sun is on the opposite side of Earth.

**Q** Can we measure a star's brightness?

**A** Yes. A star's brightness is called its magnitude. A star of magnitude 0 is very bright. Stars of magnitude 5 are only just visible. Really bright stars have minus magnitudes. Sirius, the brightest star in the sky, has a magnitude of -15.

**Q** How did sailors use the stars to find their way at night?

**A** If you live in the northern hemisphere, one star seems to stay still. This is called the Pole Star as it is almost directly over the North Pole. Sailors knew that its position showed the north, so they could then work out in which direction to sail.

**Q** Can we see the same stars throughout the year?

**A** No. Earth is orbiting the Sun, so during the year we get to see the stars all around the Sun. The Pole Star is almost directly over our Solar System, so people living in the northern hemisphere can see it all year round. For people who live in the southern hemisphere, the same is true of the Southern Cross star.

Sun

# How are stars formed?

The Sun is a yellow star. Its surface temperature is 6,000°C.

**S**tars form when hydrogen atoms in space are attracted to each other and clump together. The gas begins to burn and the star shines.

**Q** How long do stars last?

**A** The larger a star is, the shorter its life will be. Our Sun is quite small compared with some stars and has a life-span of 10 billion years. Really large stars only last for a few million years.

**Q** Are stars the same colour?

**A** No. If you look closely at stars, they are different colours. A star's colour depends on its temperature. Blue stars are the hottest. Red stars are cooler. Here are some stars and their approximate surface temperatures:

| | | |
|---|---|---|
| ● Red | up to 4,000°C |
| ● Orange | about 5,000°C |
| ○ Yellow | 5,500 - 8,000°C |
| ○ White | 8,000 - 10,000°C |
| ● Blue-white | 10,000 - 20,000°C |
| ● Blue | 20,000 - 50,000°C |

**Q** What is a supernova?

**A** A supernova is a huge star which has blown up after running out of fuel. After it explodes, the star collapses and debris is flung into space to form new stars and planets. All that is left of the supernova is a small neutron star.

**Q** What is a pulsar?

**A** A pulsar is a spinning neutron star, left behind after a large supernova explosion. It is called a pulsar because of the pulses, or flashes of energy, it sends out as it spins.

Some nebulae are made from debris left behind after supernovae have exploded (right).

Red stars are the dimmest. They are the most difficult to see.

**21**

**Q** **What is a black hole?**

**A** When a really large star explodes into a supernova, a strange thing happens. The star collapses so much that all of the material in it is squashed together. This squashed star has so much gravity that it attracts other material, even light, towards it and sucks it all in, so that it can never escape. This is called a black hole.

Black hole

**Q** **What is a white dwarf star?**

**A** At the end of their lifetimes, some smaller stars become very big and bright, before shrinking into white dwarf stars. Eventually, these white dwarf stars cool down and fade away.

**Q** **What are quasars?**

**A** Quasars are tiny star-like objects far away in space. We can only see them because they give out so much energy. Astronomers are still not sure exactly what they are!

**Q** **What are wandering stars?**

**A** Wandering stars are actually planets. We can see five planets - Mercury, Venus, Mars, Jupiter and Saturn - from Earth without a telescope. These planets look as if they are wandering about in the sky.

A planisphere is a star chart you adjust to show which stars are in the sky on any night of the year.

# What is a constellation?

**A** constellation is a pattern of stars. Ancient astronomers found that constellations were easier to recognise than individual stars. These constellations were given names.

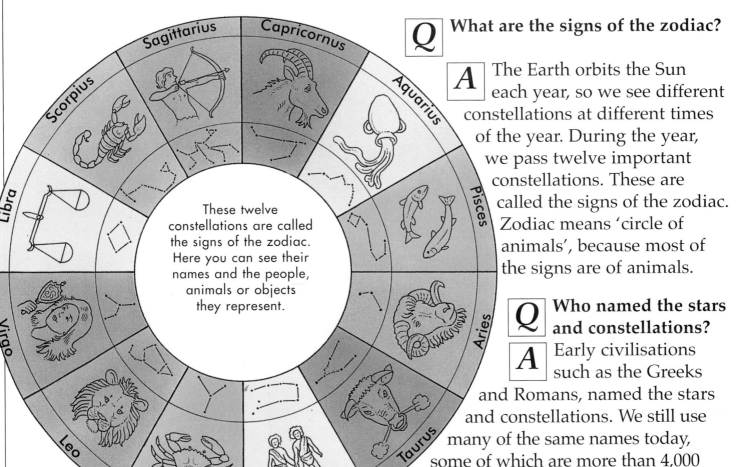

These twelve constellations are called the signs of the zodiac. Here you can see their names and the people, animals or objects they represent.

**Q** What are the signs of the zodiac?

**A** The Earth orbits the Sun each year, so we see different constellations at different times of the year. During the year, we pass twelve important constellations. These are called the signs of the zodiac. Zodiac means 'circle of animals', because most of the signs are of animals.

**Q** Who named the stars and constellations?

**A** Early civilisations such as the Greeks and Romans, named the stars and constellations. We still use many of the same names today, some of which are more than 4,000 years old.

**Q** Do constellations change shape?

**A** Yes. It takes millions of years for Earth to orbit the centre of the Milky Way. As our planet travels through space, we slowly get a different view of the stars. About 100,000 years ago, the Plough constellation looked quite a different shape.

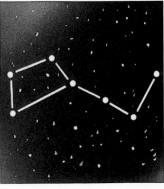

100,000 years ago

Now

There are 88 constellations which can be seen during the year in different parts of the world.

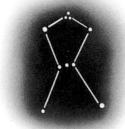

The constellation called Orion can be seen from both the northern and the southern hemisphere.

## Q What is astrology?

**A** Astrology claims to predict the future using the positions of the planets. Astrologers believe that the planets may signal good or bad luck as they move into each sign of the zodiac.

Here, Venus is in the Scorpio constellation.

## Q What is a planetarium?

**A** A planetarium is a place where you can see stars and planets projected onto the inside of a large dome. A lecturer can show you the stars' positions during the night and throughout the year. When you visit a planetarium, it is just like watching the night sky without having to sit outside!

Planetarium

## Q Are the stars in each constellation the same distance from Earth?

**A** No. The stars in a constellation may look as if they are all the same distance from Earth. Some may be only a few light years away, while others may be hundreds or even thousands of light years away.

Betelgeuse

Rigel

Orion Nebula

These stars in the Orion constellation are all different distances from Earth:

| | |
|---|---|
| Betelgeuse | 586 light years away |
| Rigel | 880 light years away |
| Orion Nebula | 1600 light years away |

## Q Is astrology the same all over the world?

**A** No. Instead of using the positions of the planets to make predictions, Oriental or Chinese astrology looks at how often eclipses, comets, shooting stars and supernovae occur.

Two astronomers used Newton's laws to predict the existence of Neptune. They were proved right when it was later seen in 1846.

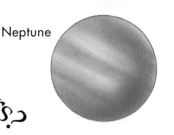

Neptune

# Who were the first astronomers?

**T**he Ancient Greeks were the first scientific astronomers. They worked out the size of Earth and that there were enormous distances between our Sun and other stars.

**Q** When were telescopes invented?

**A** Telescopes were invented at the end of the 1500s. Galileo Galilei, an Italian astronomer, was the first to use a telescope to look at the night sky. At that time, many people believed that the Sun orbited Earth. Galileo was condemned by the Church for saying that the Sun, not Earth, was the centre of the Solar System. He was, of course, correct!

Galileo Galilei

**Q** What is a radio telescope?

**A** Some objects cannot be seen with an optical telescope, but the radio waves that they give out can be detected with a radio telescope. Karl Jansky built the first radio telescope in 1932.

Radio telescope

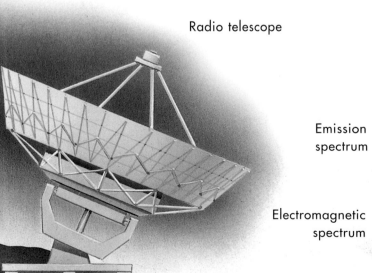

**Q** What is the electromagnetic spectrum?

**A** The electromagnetic spectrum is the range of all the energy we know about in the Universe. It stretches from wide radio waves to narrow gamma rays. Stars give out different amounts of each type of energy. This information can be recorded as a sort of bar code, called an emission spectrum. Scientists use this information to find out what materials a star is made of.

Emission spectrum

Electromagnetic spectrum

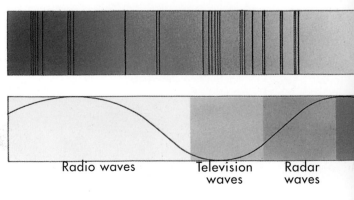

Radio waves        Television waves        Radar waves

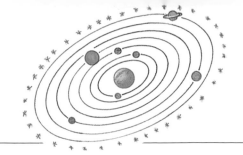

Ptolemy was a famous early astronomer who worked in Egypt. He thought that the Sun, the Moon, planets and stars in our Solar System orbited Earth.

**Q** How does a refractor telescope work?

**A** A refractor telescope uses a curved lens to bend and magnify light from distant objects, such as stars.

**Q** How does a reflector telescope work?

**A** This telescope bends light with mirrors. It was invented by scientist Sir Isaac Newton in 1668.

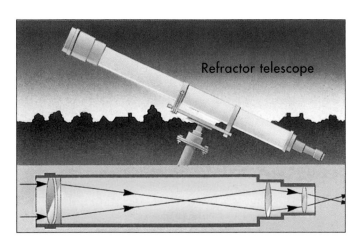

Refractor telescope

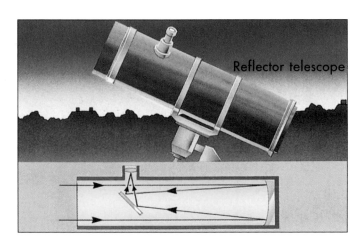

Reflector telescope

**Q** Which is the most powerful optical telescope in the world?

**A** This is a reflecting telescope with a mirror that measures 6 m across. It weighs 70 tonnes and is housed at the Zlenchukskya Observatory in the Russian Caucasus Mountains. The Keck telescope in Hawaii is bigger, but is made up of several hexagonal mirrors joined together like a honeycomb.

If a colour appears on a star's emission spectrum, that star is giving out a particular type of energy. Black lines show that some types of energy are not given out.

**Q** Who discovered gravity?

**A** Sir Isaac Newton discovered the force of gravity in 1665. Gravity is a pulling force that keeps the stars and planets in their orbits. Earth's gravity stops the Moon from floating away into space. The Sun's gravity keeps all the planets in our Solar System in orbit around it.

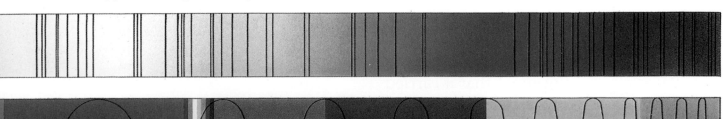

Microwaves    Infrared waves    Visible light    Ultraviolet rays    X-rays    Gamma rays    Cosmic rays

The Space Shuttle orbits Earth at 28,000 km/h.

# Earth's gravity is so strong that rockets are needed to propel satellites and other spacecraft out of the atmosphere and into space.

**Q** How does a rocket work?

**A** If a balloon is filled with air and then released, it speeds along - a rocket works in the same way. A mixture of hydrogen and oxygen fuel explodes all the time, pushing hot gas out of the back of the rocket and propelling it along.

**Q** What are satellites?

**A** Satellites are space vehicles which orbit our planet. They can relay television, radio and telephone signals around Earth. Some satellites give us weather forecasts, and others look for evidence of resources, such as oil, hidden beneath Earth's surface.

**Q** Which was the first satellite?

**A** The first satellite was *Sputnik 1*, launched in Russia on 4th October 1957. It stayed in orbit for only 90 days. The only equipment that it carried was a radio transmitter, so that scientists could track its position from Earth.

Sputnik 1

**Q** What happens to rockets after launching a spacecraft?

**A** Rockets are only needed for the first few seconds of a spacecraft's journey. They then fall back down to Earth, land in the sea and are recovered by special ships.

The fuel tank holds 2 million litres of fuel to power the orbiter's own rockets.

The rocket boosters give the Shuttle extra push for the lift-off. They fall off only 30 seconds into the flight.

A spacecraft has to travel at 40,000 km/h to escape Earth's atmosphere.

Some satellites always stay above the same part of Earth. These are usually weather satellites.

There are heat-resistant tiles on the orbiter that stop it from bursting into flames when it re-enters Earth's atmosphere.

The orbiter is attached to the fuel tank and rocket boosters for the launch. It needs no fuel to glide back to Earth after its mission.

The orbiter's rockets give most of the power to push it out of Earth's atmosphere.

**Q** **How do spacecraft land back on Earth safely?**

**A** Spacecraft such as *Apollo* and *Soyuz* both land in the sea when they come back to Earth. However, the Space Shuttle is specially designed to land like a normal aeroplane on a runway.

**Q** **Can spacecraft be re-used?**

**A** Until 1981, all spacecraft were only used once, but new types of craft such as the American Space Shuttle and the Russian *Buran* shuttle can be used over and over again.

**Q** **Where are spacecraft built?**

**A** American spacecraft, such as the Space Shuttle and *Saturn V*, are built in the largest scientific building in the world. This is the Vehicle Assembly Building (VAB) at the Kennedy Space Center in Florida. The VAB's doors are 140 m high, so spacecraft can be rolled out.

Vehicle Assembly Building, Florida

Russian astronauts are called cosmonauts.

# Yuri Gagarin from Russia was the first man in space on 12th April 1961. In 1963, Valentina Tereshkova became the first woman to be launched into space.

**Q How many astronauts have been to the Moon?**

**A** A total of 12 astronauts have landed on the Moon in spacecraft called *Apollo 11, 12, 14, 15, 16 and 17*. Unfortunately, Apollo 13 had many technical problems and its lunar module was unable to land. The crew had to fly the damaged spacecraft using the stars' positions as a guide. They landed safely back on Earth.

**Q What was the first living thing to go into space?**

**A** A dog called Laika was the first living being to go into space. Laika was launched on the *Sputnik 2* mission. Sadly, she died from panic and overheating hours after take off.

**Q What is a space station?**

**A** A space station is a large spacecraft which stays in orbit around Earth. Scientists can live and work there for long periods of time. The Russian *Mir* Space Station was launched in 1986.

**Q How do astronauts train?**

**A** Astronauts have special training to prepare them for the feeling of weightlessness in space. Before their flight, astronauts often rehearse space experiments and missions underwater. A swimming pool is filled with very salty water, which makes the astronauts float as if they were in space.

In space, weightlessness makes it very difficult to eat meals off plates. Instead, astronauts suck food out of tubes.

Without the pull of Earth's gravity, people become about 2 cm taller in space!

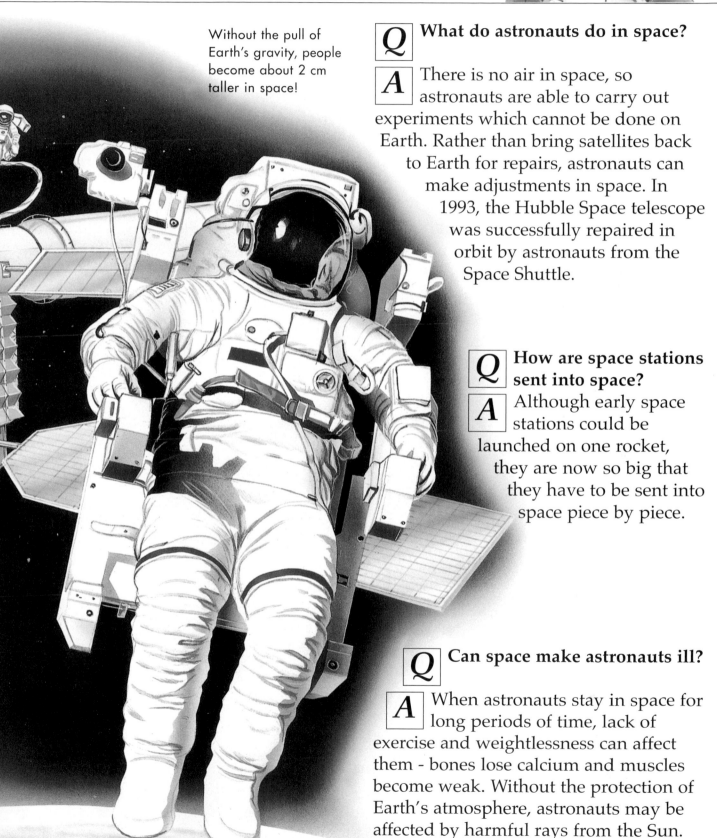

**Q** **What do astronauts do in space?**

**A** There is no air in space, so astronauts are able to carry out experiments which cannot be done on Earth. Rather than bring satellites back to Earth for repairs, astronauts can make adjustments in space. In 1993, the Hubble Space telescope was successfully repaired in orbit by astronauts from the Space Shuttle.

**Q** **How are space stations sent into space?**

**A** Although early space stations could be launched on one rocket, they are now so big that they have to be sent into space piece by piece.

**Q** **Can space make astronauts ill?**

**A** When astronauts stay in space for long periods of time, lack of exercise and weightlessness can affect them - bones lose calcium and muscles become weak. Without the protection of Earth's atmosphere, astronauts may be affected by harmful rays from the Sun.

# How can you find out more?

**NASA**

**V**isiting a planetarium, joining an astronomy club or looking round a science museum are just a few of the ways you can find out more about space.

**Q** Are there plans for any more space stations?

**A** Yes. An American space station called 'Freedom' is planned, but the enormous cost means that the project has been postponed several times. If *Freedom* ever does get off the ground, it will probably link up with the Russian *Mir* space station, allowing Russian and American astronauts to work together in space.

Mir-Freedom space station link planned for the future

**Q** How can we see further into space?

**A** Earth's atmosphere blocks out many of the rays which come from distant objects in the Universe. The Hubble Space Telescope was sent above the atmosphere so that scientists could have a clearer view and see further into space. Other instruments, such as radio telescopes, could also be sent into space to find out more about the Universe.

**Q** How far have spacecraft travelled into space?

**A** The *Pioneer 10* space probe has travelled the furthest distance. It flew past Pluto in 1986 and is still heading out into deep space!

Pioneer 10 space probe

Pluto

Captain John Young has been into space more than anyone else. He has flown on 6 space flights.

One of the next planned space missions is a trip to Mars. NASA hopes to send astronauts there in the next 50 years.

**Q** **Have we received any messages from space?**

**A** Not yet! Scientists have been listening for messages from space for years, but so far none have been received. As far as we know, signals can only be sent at the speed of light. If there were alien beings in other solar systems, they would be so far away that any messages we received from them would be thousands or even million of years old by the time they reached us.

**Q** **Can anyone be an astronaut?**

**A** When space travel first began, astronauts were all specially trained aeroplane pilots. Now, however, astronauts can be experts from different sciences who are sent into space to carry out experiments. However, competition is so fierce that as well as being science experts, hopeful astronauts also have to be lucky enough to be chosen!

**Q** **Have any messages ever been sent into space?**

**A** Yes. In 1977, two probes called *Pioneer 10* and *Pioneer 11* were launched into space. They each carried a plaque (see below) with information about our planet. Each plaque showed pictures of human beings and also space maps which gave directions to the Sun and showed the position of Earth in our Solar System.

Message onboard Pioneer probes

**Q** **How do you become an astronomer?**

**A** Anyone can study the night sky! You can stargaze from your back garden and even a small telescope gives a better view of the stars. Astronomers usually study astronomy, mathematics, physics or another science at university, and work in observatories around the world as part of their training.

# Index